When a young man's cold hand grabbed mine as I entered the Square through the Talaat Harb barricade, I yelled at him so he let me through without controlling my national identity card number.

Safaa Fathy
from "Snapshots"

SANCTUARY
(Addenda)

Anne Waldman

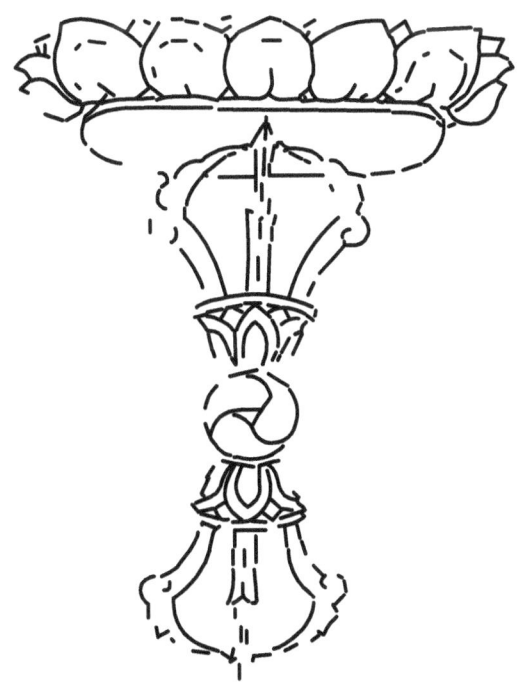

Spuyten Duyvil
New York City
2020

ACKNOWLEDGMENTS

With thanks to Shiv Mirabito for his edition of "Ceremonies in the Gong World," Shivastan Publishing, Woodstock, NY and Kathmandu, Nepal, 2007, a text cannabalized for bits for *Outrider* and *The Iovis Trilogy*. Thanks to Peter Carlaftes, Kat Georges and Three Rooms Press for "Hannah Takes Out Her Scissors" in their Surrealist Anthology. "At Mountain" appeared in The Appalachian Journal, 2018. Correspondence and notes gathered, edited and addended herein by TT & AW.

Photos by Anne Waldman contributing to collage work from the following protests:
    Climate March, NYC, 2018
    Squat, Grenada, Spain, 2018
    Rocky Flats Community Meeting, Boulder, CO, 2019
    Mexico City, disappeared students from Ayotzinapa. Poster, Mexico City 2019
    Graffiti, Ponte dell' Accademia, Venice, Italy, 2019
    Students for Justice in Palestine, Washington Square Park, 2019

Photos compliments of Lisa Jarnot:
    Fox News Action, Extinction Rebellion, "Alligators," NYC, Oct, 2019

Additional thanks to: Ammiel Alcalay, Zoe Brezsny, Ambrose Bye, Fast Speaking Music, Chris Fischbach, Natalia Gaia, Emily Harvey Foundation, Laird Hunt, Lannan Foundation (Marfa), Kiki Smith, Rodrigo Toscano, Vermont Studio Center.

    © 2020 Anne Waldman
    ISBN 978-1-949966-74-9 hdc | 978-1-949966-65-7 pbk
    Cover: Tod Thilleman (TT) design/collage with photographs by Natalia Gaia from the ICE Detention Center Protest July 13, 2019, in Aurora, Colorado.
    P. 118, Photo of Torcello, Santa Maria Assunta, "Last Judgement" (detail)

    Library of Congress Cataloging-in-Publication Data

    Names: Waldman, Anne, 1945- author.
    Title: Sanctuary : Addenda : w/ notes in correspondence/ Anne Waldman.
    Description: New York City : Spuyten Duyvil, 2020.
    Identifiers: LCCN 2019047194 | ISBN 9781949966749 (hardcover) | ISBN 9781949966657 (paperback)
    Subjects: LCGFT: Poetry.
    Classification: LCC PS3573.A4215 S26 2020 | DDC 811/.54--dc23
    LC record available at https://lccn.loc.gov/2019047194

Sung Devotions
Moon in Aries
Ceremonies In The Gong World
Hannah Takes Out Her Scissors
Suffragette
At Mountain
Donald Judd's Amygdala
Carve a Naught
Connect the Dots
Crypsus
from the Eclipse -sing) Documents
Light Coda Occludes
Truth or Consequences
The Rojava Revolution

notes & correspondent Addenda

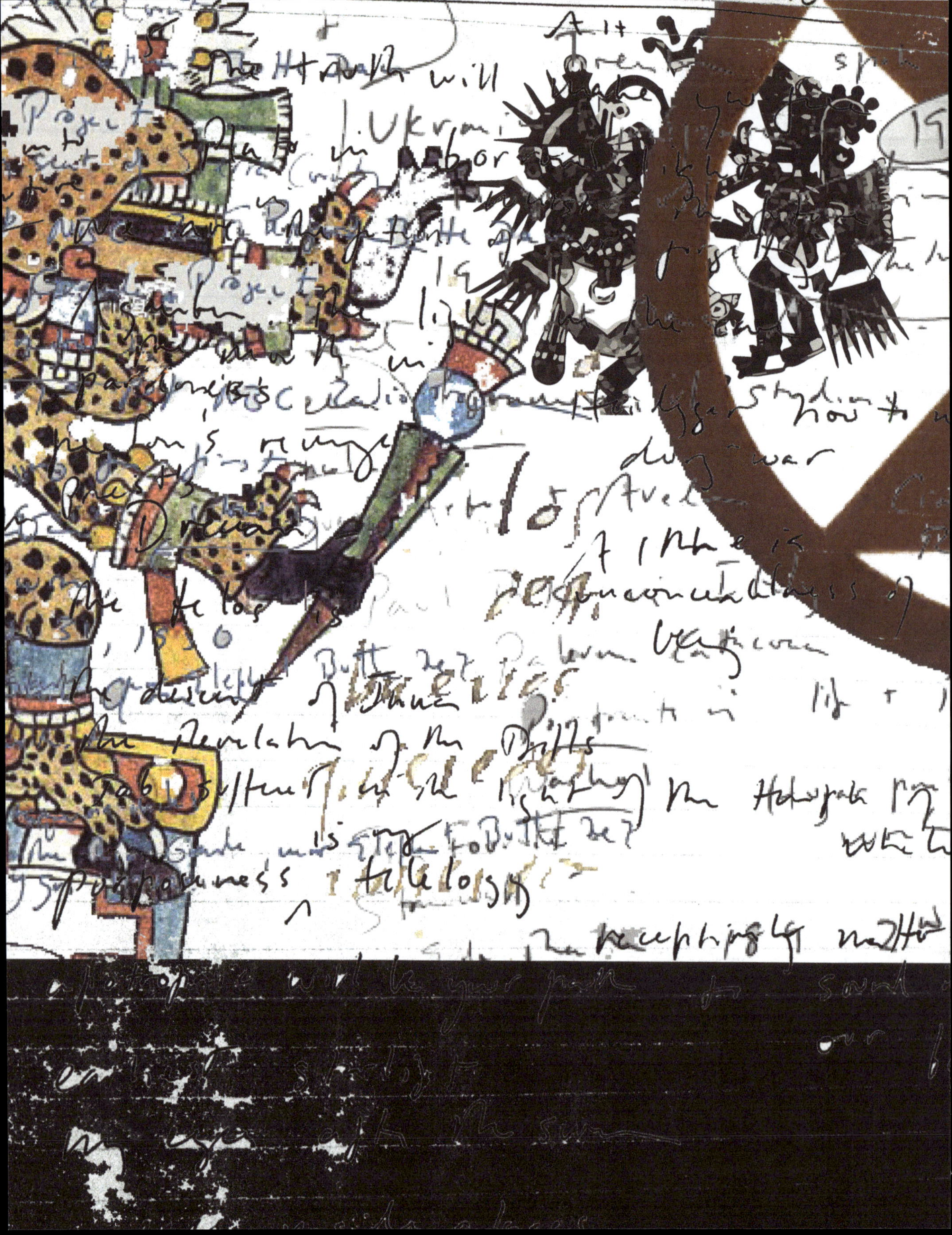
will
The telos is
purposiveness
teleology
how to
war

Sung Devotions

Could not stop as drift, mind's opalescent rhythm to land here, poetry, the war 'gainst patriarch's hold, and yet attend old men's mentor verse, IOVIS. I-OWE-THIS in the trouble times, complicity and refusal, find words to match so you won't go mad. Because you see layers of diasporas, dislocations that suffered and out of shining kingdoms, lights of Asia and deep gnosis and civilizations that soar and ashes of betrayal and genocide and the blows and shackles and hangings that mourn and make ritual and song of these. Go down these monsters! Honor the epic litany which is story of tribes' notation as we whirl and age… that we add to it, tell it best we can, humble and angered for the decimation of species and become true archons of what went down. USA post-modern poetics or minimalism on the desert stage. Leave hints of your ceremonies in shapes of clouds, cleft in rock, as Tertons do. In mindstreams whatever multiverse you swarm to. Leaving now? Rather caught up to this place I grew and feel shame of. New World's incarceration. Torment on bodies. Concentration camps. Blood on hands. Indigenous first knowers-of-spirit needed, bow low. That Mexico rise again to its shimmering sainthood absent Sinaloan pathology. Its magic of augury and shaman bird flight. Please that there be a reckoning, a balance, an evolution. Please that we do not become lost in our robotic Capitalocene hell realm, our false paradise, greed and privilege, our destruction through nuke weaponry, missiles with toxic tip plutonian culpability. Our Walls. Our starvation of life, of air. Insatiable ghost realms: so very hungry! How can you love without a dream of other? Alone dying and alone together living and dying. What once could breathe. What is this version of a world? … and out of Mexico, here first, New Mexico, California, Texas. No more death death death bodies that senses be keen and sharpened that we still call out the fascists who slaughter truth and body and future, complicit in the meltdown of this human existence and spiritual mystery. That we care for our seas, our coral reefs, forests, our mountains, late in the game of harm, and we will need to catch up otherwise a dirge for the voice of Anthropos, wreck of the human. May we disappear with our fraught suicide, recede to other zones of consciousness? Do no harm. Sing and sound here.

Got another 500 years?

days of more slaughter August 3, 2019

where "chaos"
in Chaldean
  meant
without a library

Moon in Aries

   res

a kind of
reserve
 arete
  spin
  of things,

of sorts, softer light
       make this a thing
           "a moldy confluence"
tenemos *after Darwin*

 language has been locked
goes dead

in traps of appetite

needing interpreter
   hermeneus

 to contrive/to tell

play dice, the old woman
  all you could alter of her affect
in a throw   flick of the finger's
  scriptly forgetfulness, blow it off!

translates as

"fields of oscillation"

white dwarf stars & neutron stars & elementary particles

swim in Dharmakaya nimbus
coding numbers
for every possible
position
in space
a particle
could
utter
(occupy) a cranial optic scheme

   (alter) (obviate) (stutter)

astrologation chromosomes

"Rumble in the Jungle," Kinshasa
old videotape in lobby
Irian Jaya, Ali & Foreman

transplant a seed syllable
  inside your body cloth
royal robes of the Vedic Age

stay humble, boxing

 O Varani

  you must be Lady Adamantine
  for the mulling time

      (nullifying-cosmos-time)

analytically cool

as you loom down
     a suffering world, *souffrance*

mani= jewel

accessorize!

Bottled Night
Amber Word
Necklace of Chokability
Cinch of seatbelt
(unfasten
emergency exit)

a *puja* for apocalypse, Malaysia

  transform your skin as you sleep under new moon

magnetize worlds, let them go
  first precession of equinoctial love

    ram of cranial nerve out a window

How would you build yr city
at the flux of the Klang and Gombak rivers
upon earth mounds
cruxation
 'gainst mutability

what we can carry and bite of dust

                        a modern world?

Ace of Wands, your ramshackle work isn't done….

                                      [Kuala Lumpur, 1989]

Ceremonies In The Gong World

             "Senang makan nasi?" (Do you like rice?)

What sound 5 am? Processional. Leading the barong back to the temple. She-Who-Is-Away-From-Home-Again ponders the turmoil these multiheaded islands are prone to. The breakaways. Is she a breakaway island? She wants another possibility to the kingdoms of poetry, the new careerisms. She goes out to be counted. Confronted. There are legions of spies on motorbikes. She has to conceal her Noam Chomsky tapes. Bloody former battles of East Timor keep the community on pins and needles. The fires of Kalimantan rage without respite. And even more recent disasters. How many dead who spent their last minutes in incendiary auto-de-fé? Terrorist attacks at a nightclub won't change the world, just sadden the frequency. Arjuna's passion? Battles of family, of clan. Disco horror. Tsunami for a troubled coast. Aceh will never rest, someone says "unquell the world." I say "Saya namanya Anne, please let me in." Smoke gets in all our curious eyes. The rupiah is plummeting. A balian *predicts the Marxist Age of Dismemberment. I come here trembling, to remember how we studied the past to understand the future. Remember? A time when our gamelan instruments were made of iron. When we walked around barebreasted. Where the "inner temple" was alive with ancestors who now only fret and scold us. Invoke a local deity when all else fails. She is the rice you must save to feed the future. What justice? What peace?*

blandishments
an odd remorse for ataxia
is hinted at
ceremonies in the gong world
a calm one wants attention
in temple dress
out in the courtyard
lighting up by the cardboard
shrine door
black lace *kebaya* custom made for funerals

the joke being the Balinese used to dress in all the colors of the rainbow,
a funeral was a festive time
then the government (Jakarta) decided to promote black
institutionalize grief
& soon they'll be *crying* at the funerals
my lover: his radial symmetry his
jewel ornaments
his dark eye
to summon a Mata Hari
impulse
& were the deities impressed
flying over the little village?
& were they going to come down and visit
with their bows & arrows & magic bells?
Sri Dewi rules here,
you know she will arrive,
replete with humble guards
you know you know she will
arrive
rumpled
terrifically
maddened by desire
with all her rice accoutrements
and if not
the land dies
because chemicals push on for greater yield
smoke
goes up
and men shake wildly in their sarongs
o beautiful snake-charmer,
short order cook,
gorgeous diva
realms upon realms of desire keep your safe return...

dear Ammiel –
Beloved students —during manifestation of an ongoing
performance class I teach at Naropa University entitled "Liberation
Now!" fretted over the cultural imperialism and colonialism of
Antonin Artaud and Ezra Pound. Their respective white privileged "gaze"
toward Balinese and Tarahumara cultures in the case of Artaud
(although Artaud embarked on his "voyage to the land of speaking blood" to
ritually ingest peyote) and Pound helped "reveal" Japanese Noh. Is mere
literary "orientalism," an old trope, the problem here? I gave some
historical context which, while not trying to beg the issues particularly,
encouraged insight into these writers' important acts of exploration. William
Carlos Williams's "Beautiful Thing" had also recently been called into
question in its objectification of women. Ted Berrigan's use of the word
"legs," and so on. Could Gertrude Stein's own anti-Semitism be seen
perhaps as "internalized oppression"? The privilege (of "not having to
work a day job") of H.D.. Incipient racism of many of the modernists.
Charles Olson's use of the word "chink." The class and privilege and
"academizing" of Language Poetry and so on. What arose, also, was a sense
of the real "split" in the culture so obvious in the recent U.S. Presidential election
debacles where many people of color are disenfranchised and where blue-color-
white-male-ethos is undervalued in terms of the weight it carries toward a
conservative (and scary) agenda. Not to mention the dis-functionality of the party
system and so on. Where is a writing and by extension, the performance,
which includes a consideration of the whole "polis"—the civic city and
its many eyes. Impossible, one thinks. The examples of dismay are
endless when much of the avant-garde reads as elitist, operating within
very specific language and economic codes. Where to go? What is being a
poet *now* about? We *will* be happily under-the-radar, a temporary autonomous
zone where we will be gazing at the whole picture...
rather jobless,
string,
ribbon —
something
idle, cloth
with saint's weave

sweet idol of him,
masked dancer
powered round a
halo of
honor, holy
restless
nanosecond
shutter don't budge
lust's pubescent necklace
boy
I know
would never mention
lathes—
could he?
still
dim
ritual
start clacking
clanging for
tippled roar
whores chase him for
& his boyhood would
be fair gone game

a mother's thumb
concedes
against the
holy stone
vertigolichen
& hang like silk,
pale, in
the
March sun
Love,
Anne-Grasping-the-Straws-More-Tightly-Now

Because these are the postures we surmise in light…lit up in stone:
across from me is a crossing of leg, across from me the fabulous silks
which are like an intruder writing in ceremonial space, waiting…folded
in a slant way, head turned right gazing, then it goes another
way, slanted, as if to say notice this, notice this detail before you
[lose interest] [before something interrupts the ordinary obscure
paragraph] or [you stop adding on your long lines of narration] or [the
premium story of a cosmology goes pale] or [origin myth on the relative
differences between genders is falsified]
the way you receive the sun, the moon, the stars into your habitat, into
your temple zone where the psy ops can't reach ("terror" get outta here!)

Occultist wit, for that's what it seems to be, help me out here again dear witness, see a way through a chaotic time, the face of these images, turn blood to stone turn stone to fire make a limb dance toward ozone carried by a force you are capable of making a lineage picture of: dream of a dust bowl dream of a prophet dream of a soldier, a rice deity, the dawn of a pre-Raphaelite utopia, dream a Machiavellian sports announcer, dream of a future dictator, or sentence that leaves you cold, all the embers down, you have no refuge but mantra

Talk about Java now, the vision when you stood in the doorway lintel, and all did not seem strange or earthquake-prone. It was the day before the movie shoot, day before the funeral, the day before the self-immolating attack, when incendiary meant simply "hot", and you could say it about a lover: "hot" if you were so inclined, day before the discotheque folded, the day before so many were wounded, and you could make something North American about it, including all the continents that would keep a Polaris missile out of their midst, and then it all came back to you, opposite me, leaning over your instrument of power that would record an inquisitive face, not an Agrippa at the control, not a tyrant nor a super errant knight, and you might ask about threads and stitches and you might inquire about buttons and harnesses, about exigencies of destroying proof, about all colors matching, about a reversal of intention in your dance costume before the Mayan long count, the Eka Rudra calendar, before the day we might go to practice our Ramayana syllables, and good intention needs to shine on those syllables, taking them out of the bomb shelter, avaunt all paranoid behavior out of the time warp and onto the road where you stood waiting for the shutter to snap, shouting "Hold" and then it was your face that was always needed, face which was always with me and it could hold anything it wanted to, an unforced perspective, lunar calendar, resistance, way of thinking, behaving, as spectator to the spectacle, daily life

or
like the flowering sandat
(*Cananga Odorata Baill*)
which curves year round,
veining
6 wrinkled green petals
(long)
(narrow)
(limp)
(striated)

6 tentacles to hide sex behind, its visage a dot
micrometers
or seduce a curious eye
assured then
tendril-ed how
when
6 directions of
universe collapse
6 sense perceptions,
green-dream mandala
collapse

tropical zone includes being tendered in yellow
in green in yellow-green,
lemon-green, green-green
& would be fried in tumeric for golden oil
& placed on a body
a body is as ranged as far as flower is ranged
as flower is at center of speech, in that chord
that voice which is flower too and
mouth which is flower opening
ringed as far as curve is & concentrically so ringed
as far as body would love or die against
flower this one because it sends out the signal
& curves, rounded, veining, sings, ringing
I AM THAT FLOWER LANGUAGE

difficult to see because they, the syllables, occur high in this tall tree
reach up
toward scent
& offered such,
reach up to be
pinched early at the market
ripples are early at Tirtagangga as one walks there
one is in sandat, moves in sandat
market sings of sandat
& sandat is salve
for healing
& bark and twine and palm
you sculpt by hand

(because the spirit is strong like these stronger vines)
complex at center,
at vox-chord, entanglement
compound stigma
& would sweat perfume, reach up to sweeten fingers

in the bath it is the most scented
most favored
& *in my hair, this flower anoints the human realm.*

(I sang this as antidote to the fathers/warlike persistence
or tendency to ritual suicide…which is not out of the question
when the chips are down…)

To Those of You in the Sandhyabasha conversation:
Yes, the somewhat free use of the term "Sandhyabasha" doesn't come
particularly from a reading of Mircea Eliade and was never used or
recorded to my knowledge by Kerouac or Ginsberg or other con-frères.
I had my own desire to present the idea of a secret code—perhaps
intuited by other initiates (see collaboration & bebop improv of "Pull
My Daisy"). We are certainly aware of the literal definitions. Apologies
for taking poetic liberties and this only encourages me to more
"dialogue" with the left-hand path scholars. "Ulatbamsi," more literally
"upsidedown" is probably a more accurate term for what some of us yearn
to do in our poetry. And of course there's "dakini script," which is what
some poets think they're onto, not to mention the sense of the poem as
"terma," or hidden treasure (as in the Tibetan Buddhist tradition).
What do you think?

(changing the name Anne Grasping etc. to "On the Job in Indonesia")
this **poem of particles** is but
tiny integument
of
cartilage,
strangers
between
species
glue on the knuckle,
spit at tongue
groin in a moan
umbilicus cut
you are on your own now

clot at the throat,
a muscle gone down
shadows of sinewy deals,
a witchy stew
body parts (sift, sift thru them,
citizens of the world...)
enraptured by lizard,
held by design of dove,
akin to the raptor

how to pounce like a leopard
sleek and moving forward in your tight sarong
survival in a wound's tourniquet
villages in another sphere
twisting & turning?
are we on Saturn?
a new *mecca?*
you say *center of the mind is this polis*
retina collapses/sees no reason for any other
version of jungle
unstable?
meek?
rocky
liquid terrain
escape her moons?
(Mungkah Lawang)
fact, legend, magic are fuzzy
wouldn't you, too, be?
& stem from here, a whole map of desire, tyranny
the way we navigate "globally"?
or a whole gamut of characters one by one appears
at the split gate,
Chandi Bantar

are you tourist-ic
or cruel &

substantial?
perhaps relative to the periphery of chance?
epic could be considered essential
but I'm too tired for that
I'd rather be a petulant prime minister
braving the *monetary crisis*
than a god
without a shrine
to come home to.

[Ubud, 2000]

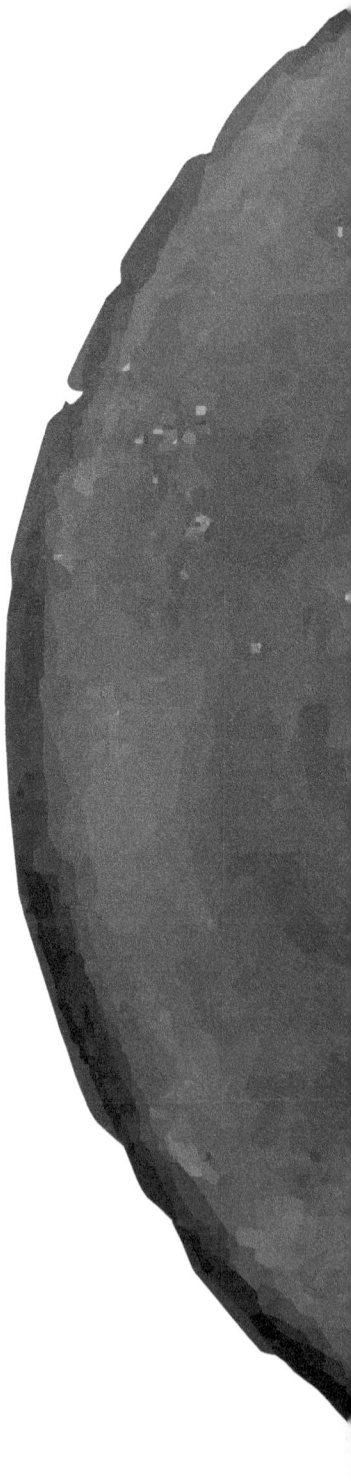

Hannah Takes Out Her Scissors

This was the time the poet returns once again to her library. Back from Hong Kong. She's feeling "memorized." Embarks on the portraits. Considers the lesbian moonlight in all times being contemporaneous. Google plans move into the neighborhood, opening offensive exec offices. When you weren't looking you could simply comment: more traffic. Dial it down. And Disney near the other end of her world, just around the corner. The floods brought on a new cartography. And the maps are in exile.

Insolence and the lovely life of
A Hannah Hoch
A rankling of affinity
Girl moods
My old rigor, my girl
Distort head & sex
Roll over
The moon the moon
See?
Fragmented the truth serum
Marx happened
Existential better be your mother
Idiocy of the curl
Churlish lip
A chuff and a chin curls
Ivory spurt
Da-Daddy
Silks and a pattern
A fluid moonlight
You only offer sandwiches beer and
Coffee? The cruel Richter
The married Raoul
Men on the slant
A chase for origins
Spools, clansfolk, adherents
Surprise!

Got Hong Kong blues?
You could be a fashion plate
Cut the A lines
Then the fish
Architectures break down
Come see me in your cutting mode
A small street in old town
Rattling vehicles
Fish heads for sale
Shopping as a guise
Checking out investments
Vestibules relegate the downturn
Collecting culture on a downswing
The little pieces of paper! Aha!
On the verticals
Crass deformations
Caress a transient metabolism
The new multi-territories of identity
I will vote only in my anarchist bones
Skin over, sing over the melody
Bring the vocals up,
My bone my bones, bring them on
Abrupt denial's tension
My larynx hungers for your not-art?
Are you not-culture? Not you?
What are you?
Knot of Hannah, wired to montage
This is my camera: China
Hannah leaves the café
Warmer, less hungry
She goes into zone B
Traffic where zone A is all cars
World War I is a Red Cross
My fellow sisterly feeling
Then I go into exile, dear girl
My exchange for Mao money
Don't speak for my world, World!

Is news fascination?
Can she travel? She will stay in Berlin
Nazi down the block
Hannah hocks the tribal feeling
Hannah takes out her scissors
Punishing fears of rhythm dominance
Cut cut the ghosts
Cut cut linear time
Cut modernity!
Cut the men who dissolve
Birds & wings & snakes
Cut cut cut
Artifacts resume power and
Prevail to alter a work station
Music elevated to the
Fetish on a badly missionized street
Are you memorized yet?
Memorialized?
Is intervention a plus for you?
Skip rope, and hope hovers
Then you're bodied
You are hooded
Waiting for the ax to fall
Get high up, don't make it be all you!
About the money, about love
Waiting for flood relief in the dark age
Encounter a detour, a woman's glove
Memory needs objects
Mountains are frozen waves
Image de la Chine?
We overlap you, my girl, my Asian cartoon
Alive in my roaring time frame
Text your observers my way
Need better reportage
Your salvaging status, Hannah
Held in the lockdown
On the wildlife dial

Oral tribes in your astrology chart?
Gunning & truck lore?
Today it's also armed trucks
Border patrols, armed vigilantes
Lockdown, mass death
Today it's a critical mass
Of violence and suffering
Thousands in the streets
Document sent for "too few"
Immigrants, no room
The sunshades give silence
But wake up the sleeves!
Uncoil Berlin!
Die Braut!
Germany welcomes you!
Uncoil New York
Are you vertical?
Empire of cutting up outlier China
Un-reconcilable
Our new world Weimar
Mantra of montage
Don't violate city anthropology
Text your massive hope: 2020
We learn from you
Images not sacrosanct
Epic rainbow struggles
Lost in shoes a global destiny
Then get out of my way
Headband regalia?
Starve the puritans, rattle their cages
Will guide you
Loop waver fork
Don't mimic the lost bodies
They need your cut cut deranged eyes.

[Berlin/NYC, 2019]

TODAS LAS OPRESIONES ESTÁN CONECTADAS

TRANSFEMINISMO INTERSECCIONAL

***If you could just see us now**, in servitude. If you could just see how we're still jumping hoops. If it hadn't happened if it never and merely was to happen who report to here? What is time, a multi-thread gorgon. The beginning is the past identity in a feminist woe. In queer woe. In trans substantial woe. I wanted to go back & visit with my dying sisters and to storm out of the cloisters. Look at my confrères in the lineup Stonewall just down the road. St. Christopher Street. How groans with sisters I could rally with. What it's like to be in the consummation of heat and love. It was freedom we would fight for. Love and spin and dance around freedom. We're performing in the Trans Squat in Grenada tonight, laughter and tears.*

Suffragette

Future Suffragette move closer, her trial a trail of ratification and progress. Never halt, more words. Justice, expediency. Suffragette argues, a speech of any one woman's life. Would a ballot protect you? Resounding. And family. I cannot eat or wear the money he brings home each payday. Give me political status. I do not eat the home, I cannot eat the house. I will lie down and read my books. I will write another *tractus*.

A long upswing panting for, if *he* differ how *they* differ from each other. From men. The great sanctuary is the gate of women.

Those who study the sturdy oak about which the ivy clings find it dead at the top. Suffragette minimus walks, suffragette minimus shows up, suffragette minimus attempts to convince the fence-sitter.

Study the root systems, nesting within nestings.

Suffragette notes the new immigrants use Sunday for recreation. They drink, women work outside the home, they rarely live in big houses on tree-lined streets, but prefer the overcrowded tenements in which Mother could rarely be Queen of her home. Suffragettes note this and complain. And help the poor immigrant.

Suffragette minimus complaint of steerage. Compliant, literacy test?

Debates. Taxpayers. Standing alone. Standing in unison. Foreign borners joining suffrage organizations. Numbers swell. O my workers!

How do we categorize the impact of the black man? Abolition a cause, and surely, abolition a cause. Progressive era, a secret like Eleusis.

Eleusis embellishing the ranks....

At Mountain

Germination: place, time, how rare, you realize, of sacred word sites.

    Where is Hitler
      1933?

    Getting more than started

    Austria
    murky,
      com
    promised
    place,

      getting rejected
      if not art school
      it's "life"
      perennial master

      the mastiff
      a matador   somewhere
      then Mussolini drives the
          notes down The Lateran Pact

    murder-camps to come

    hideous remembrance
      short cut to cold stars

    could you whistle could you paint
      could talk?

     Surely, very here, thirties-fifties-

John Dewey
a praxis
   hands on

Where shelter?

What sense perception affords you
 Ezra's hall of mirrors
a pound of flesh

Locked in
    truce your body
   ne'er be ill served this watch

then
    bundle your being
for
a fascist enterprise

              fashia weak
  ancestors in coma

no one a villain, but everyone
when you
remember "the times"

what we are up against

 needs: foundation
          consciousness
How rare
  you are yet to be born
  inside
     PTSD of the father

WWII

...girlhood
on the bomb
a wandering a wand a great forgetting

"Downtown NY in NC"
(did Franz Kline say that?)

Albers?
    Anni
  Got out

Needs: visionaries
 all bare witness
    voice in wilderness
   sting of it
above humiliation

And welcoming here O
   come to this Eden
creating art falling out of Eden

(meaning renegades,

or up starts the panic
or seed will grow   now

get ready for

green grass
 allowance in discourse

mix it up   neutrinos like
     partners

 allies   "work duty"

    lovers)

on this mountain
  already cut a path
nay could rest placid
tranquil
      blasting spells
ideas but in reasonings

  in but word the adequate symbols

that you remember
need not war to make it new

so must build
inside war machine

PRIMORDIAL STUPA

Where is the mind
  of civilization not
in
fogs
of
war

 Where is Jim Crow?
(next door)

Where is poetry?
  in rhythms of its legacy
& now
all the figures of Outward

Ed Dorn (born under a dark star)

Creeley ("when I speak, I speaks")

John Wieners, a man who became one with his poetry

& Fee Dawson with Dan Rice, "the effect on us of Franz…"

  Youth in shadows of
replacement
  who's
what
in fact
  here
real bodies?

      Real Depression?

Magic and witchy lore
     in rural modernism

Be a mountain
  of evidence
 How brave

Be chronicler
Of moment
Clime and you burst

 The air so high here

came
before
marched
this

way
feeling
lighter
than the
times

so young Dorn would come
& young Creeley
& young Wieners & Fielding
& Olson impossible
administrator

"running a school out of a car"

then possible patriarchy
impossible gnosis
out of what vehicle to create
Kulchur
is this

polis is (also) this ?

[Boone, NC, 2017]

Donald Judd's Amygdala

The color in situ
It—color—parallels in situ
I wanted all the colors to be present at once
In place it resolves it solves
It revolves
Devolves absolves fear
In place, it says I am placed thus
In pure unconditioned but adjudicated space
With tug of form
In space it says start with a dot in space
A formation of boxes in situ
In site rendered by chance
By accountability
By prefabrication
By the cool interior of distant waters
By the hues of quiescence
By dim light of
Receptacles of color in place in situ
Hold hold hold
Contain
Beat and enameled into certain hues
Pare it down
Pare it down
Down (sits down in meditation posture)

In tandem
In comparison
In contract
In agreement
In resistance
In conversation
In situ the conversation

Placed by eyes, by arms, you cannot
Sit on these
But you could sit inside color
A container for dwelling in concept
No no resist resist concept
Resist symbology
Dwelling in an abstract context
Far from drama
Far from passion
Where box is a listening device where it could hold your life force
Where you could adorn and delineate space
Add to and counting
(aside) 1 a form 2 a form 3 a form 4 a form 5 a form 6 a form 7 a form
Subtract
7 a form minus 6 a form minus 5 a form minus 4 a form minus 3 a form minus 2 a form minus 1
What I thought of was the stacking I needed
Was the organization I needed to be stacked of
In stacking I needed
A fast track
To stack within
The sleek apparatus of now
The sleeker priority of urge
To make a form
An addition of numbers
8 a form 9 a form 10 a form 11 a form 12 a form
To stay in the loops of
Making it work
Hammering and cutting
And nailing
And resistance of material
The warrior's metal
The armor of form
For pristine edges and corners
For the cool seduction of metal
Risk of metal
Demand of metal

That cools in the heat
For my thought to enter this one
A state of mind of aggression
A state of equanimity
A state of exaltation
Didn't want combinations be too harmonious
Nothing remiss
Nothing is missing
There is pleasure to the eye
Because eye is absorbing clarity
And intention of building
If the ideas were stacked what would the sequence be
You say a red thought you say a blue thought is enamel pleasing?
Is it reassuring does it matter
Can you love without it
How does it sound arid and abed?
I wanted all the colors to be present at once
How does it keep you within itself
How utilitarian is it to your mind
Form is emptiness, emptiness is norm
Eschew all formulas in the spiritual realm
Could you say you saw to say this is a raw color?
Would you say deep, saw raw?
Your hippocampus
I didn't want to combine
I didn't want the colors to combine
Your amygdala I would intersperse this with polemic
With theory
I will not be ignorant of intention
The artist who is author
I would collect inside these chambers I would offer my sharp
Color system which has a psychology all its own
What is a bombing of Syria to this question
To minimalists who survived Hiroshima
No confusion between the anthropomorphic and the abstract
Increased collaboration
There is no Father Space or Mother Space
Space is nothing and we are brittle

And elusive
A formal logic of crystallography
Antimatter consciousness of structure which maintains a remote distance from the organic
The "unconscious" has no place in his art
His crystalline state of mind is far removed from the organic floods of
"action painting"
Translates his concepts into artifices of fact, without any illusionistic representations
Ups are downs and downs are ups
Increasing hardness
Geological formations
A   throw   obscene
I wanted multiplicity all at once
Anthro
   Pocked   Seen
Nothing not intercede upon
By the hand of man

Brought space down into an abstract world of mineral forms
No progressions
Not represent anything
In my auditory imagination

Fascination fabrication
As in a glass jar held in hand
You turn it around and around

You mix the elixis in the alembic
Forged of aluminum
For lightness and subtle power line

Australian aborigines take 40 years
To become songmen
Memorizing epic material that covers
A cycle of migration
It might take 20 – 40 years and your poem will
Tell of this
A well as the total botany of an area
And where the water holes hide…

Tradition that could be 12,000 years old

Time has many anthropomorphic representations,
Such as Father Time, but space has none
What holocaust could rock this power house of emptiness?

2. Around and around

what holocaust could rock a notion of disappearance
tension and balance in my mood of him

what is conceded recedes in a mood of him
strict rules against illusion and falsity

3. Fathers of time

increasing hardness
deposits from the mind
as Smithson says: 1965

brought I down brought we down brought they down brought
down space
brought abstract space down to the minimal for
I brought down
We brought down
They brought down
We brought down
She brought down
Did they bring down?
Did I bring down?
Did you bring down?
Did the palace move?
Did the ice palace crumble?
Did they bring down Mendieta?

Did we they he she it and all of us move space?
What is the generation that says these things?
Father Time
And space has none of they?

Father Time
And we look up in our theisms

There is no Father Space or Mother Space

Space is nothing but plurality

Why vague? Why faith?
Elusive and brittle

Crystallography
Abstract crystal as a solid

Bounded by symmetrical simplicity

The entire box would collapse
Without the tension of the axe's
Downs are ups and ups are down

No confusion between the anthropomorphic and
The abstract

The unconscious has no place in art
Concepts translated into artifices of fact
Without any illusionistic representations

Antimatter
Antimatter

Resistance in the metabolic biosphere

Antimatter

Anti matter

Antimicassser

Anti aster
Anti at her
At here the color come to meet the dream
That is resolute and sleek
& preternatural

proprioception

4. El Greco

El Greco
What do you think of when I say this?

The angles of clarity?
A gaunt face
Color that is a spectrum unto itself

It's odd, the color.

El Greco
Echo El Greco

5. Lonely

lonely
lonely
lonely
lonely

word spin
a little orb
in dark space

6. lonely

lonely
speak to me I say

7. Kiki Smith says at teatime:

can't use that word minimal
but a clear lucid aesthetic
anti-decorative
no appendages
no weepy twigs
no people but when they enter the space
they are people and then they are no longer people

it makes you wonder: people? really?

Decoration comes in with women
Late 1800s
Form following function
Invention of computer
Not different strength and line
By information carried

Big theories
Big theories
Culture incorporates
Could it have been Calvin Klein with Donald Judd?

It happens in line and form

Judd's furniture
Vienna

(aside) (*I notice he disses your father*)

8. What is an artist's relationship to 'istorin?

That is always a quest and a question

I am not initiated, Kiki says
Sculpture that can resemble jewelry
Elemental but ornamental
Obsession
(aside) (*I wonder could this be another gender construct
60s plexiglass*)
Canal Street, you know, Larry Bell…
Paul Thek, Allan Shields
Something totally different on the heels of
Judd
And color?
Color is a spectrum of logic and then surprise

Judicial
Judicious

Judicate
Generate
In the turbine of the cold storage
& the hot color
walking around
colors I had never seen working their way into the eye
and its happy reflection back but
with a subdued emotion

you can be happy with your own emotion
when you are satisfied…

within the containers of sound and sight
vibrations in inimitable, restless
striving—for void
making and disappearing
room in the room in the room you show
and live?

in?

A kind of fabulous scary domination

[St. Louis Pulitzer Foundation
--->
Marfa, 2017]

Carve A Naught

ask
   & be gone
dignitas
                       "the hearings"

  gravity of
countenance

effigies
that I had a book
once
in penance

takes blur
  off bygone

& augur's ornament

 a sum
of
personal
  clout
that
 a
male
citizen
acquires
throughout
lifetime

sung:
 when my bridge comes down
 when my bridge my bridge cometh down

   and wait aye over
trellis:

   the lout

of all, this was the needles

     then
 old staves

what then, laddie?

shelter entrance
 in the dim
above

gauge boots on the ground

       gruff troll

 infernal gulag boots on the dole

noxious

         rue a court

ring a bell
    rug a person into
curt prison cell

volumes handed out
at recess

Saturn a bum's rush
      Satyr's day

  press my cap
Bless me
lest go mad!
arrest me
  with *autoritas*

ask and be warned

P of performance
peril
   piety
 perfection

P of perfidy

per fidem decipere

   deceive
thru

trustingness

but who ever?
Be,

    foresworn?

ask to
     see the world
without us,

        iron door

   inner chambers

    then the preps

      text you from heil hell

   in witch light burning

       meontic

stop meshing
  clear
severance

    it will all be rust

it's the day

alone
  dark door
convention

         mashing
 predict the
kali yuga

   rape of virgins

   it's the back room day

   small coy nouns
  a rare triangle
for devils

speak in poems
      beholden to
  nightingales
fin d'amor
is what we do

          it's the day
wreck on
 topoeisis
            dictions
for uncommon Todorov

a healing grotto

     thousands of years ago

Zeus's bull-cart

or some such
   fuck 'em,

it's the day
in my exile
outside
   the capital

 & world comes up
   out of
glade
dripping
 with
mans-
    plaining

vernaculars

 achtober 6, anno domini
taking shit
 from the silver spoon

   it's the day the fix is in

"it ain't dead"

                    nominee no man cloture

            it's a day vanished volumes

  only this possible now
failure of strategies
        succumbs
La Moule
  and fail fiefdom?

Medusa
Octopi

        no one is perfect

only this
   Roland song
was born
        & killed

rhythm dismantles borders
   cretan memories (he)

against stanzas
   a bleak courage (she)

I am sick and must fain lie down

over spirits
        made
   dunes
      but but but but but but

it's the day (they)

overtime

    made my runes

rhizome's terminus

    how soon be gliding?

came to taste the
  virgin

honey
  renewed
without
  complaint

over body made her ruins
  & she rise

in the cupboard
 a
lash

 the
future
already in

entrails

 and she rise

words were clouds
  were morgue-sweepers

   meeting to

drive on genocide
  to whisk out
  the poor

thought what
you said-
when?
meaning
   under wrap
non spoken was
original "women"?
you thought, long over,
   primitivo?

thots that rise

put
monsters under control
 let's just see how to
top a bend

 on yr river line
  echo of speed rustle

              hussle

diviners under control
put
hoof lore
  little pessimisms
 on the sea rim
 hustling
   receptivity

in role of surveyors
false or derivative

 this
what wurmed in
the senate

loaded the day
gravity is the
 collaboration

call lab oration
    curtain
and a wall

beginning & starting again

   justice

find me
    in gender
vulnerability the action
Dr. Christine Blasey Ford's
  defeat

     but kicking

       found
          on
that
stair

     case

 rise
    to
carve a
    naught

[Gihon River ("bursting forth," "gushing"
out of the Garden of Eden)----->Vermont, 2018]

Connect the Dots:

rigpa tsephep

(insight reaching its full measure)

image
in
nation

"transparency"

mercurial
dakinis   . . .

 Robin to
    catch us   in a blaze

"..so memory can step across…."
                                        apocalypse
dream rooms, serial marriage
         the coming community
candelaria's high
capital's

Huichol's
higher

   up
in the mischief of *brujas*..
   chain of command
    so they make a person disappear

   on the rim of Irreparable

The poet in
     long Bolinas night   lost
his leather coat for

the woman on the rafters

waving her witchy twig

dawn, the science
   unthinkable old breakdowns

     smoked her will

but did it rue or wail the bedouin

 memory is a spell

   body aligned in image's alliance?

shelter whispers

    "wants"

 really hear?

phylon, crucible for you

 survival tact
   in defiance

    and now
nor
between nor ever

        Mueller
    & a hard place
voyage of
dirt realms

 and bandy words in the mysteries: FBI

how togte pqabk squawkbelt to craquelld claquer plack erd

    did we think "the lonely enclosure of history?"

 did blue Tara come down from her perch
and be sambhogakaya double agent

    for all the melancholic babes?

abstracted identity collapsing   into sex   scandal

  and silence,

  great lap or lapse of world swollen with generosity

    a horn in her hand.
truth bell in the other

and forests became labyrinths for the sport
& sound

a handbell choir

    when you outwit intelligence ops

red

herring

derring do

        was paved with

mercury retrograde
              for a "gentlemen's agreement"
crossroads
  melting into bigger *kayas*
& more when
Valery sleeps

 Or Dame Wariness

en cry pt shun

crypts
for
asking a point

   the hidden:

     and tears before the crypt of Jonas Mekas

"like he just steeped out for a walk"

              meek as a sprite

with porcelain hands at rest

palms of tribute

they rise to wave
  every so steady now waving

like the seaweed down under where

  bones of coral made
mudra of blessing

   what a slice of silver time

a puncture, my centuries

are you actual or
ethereal
  as you go? dear meekness

pinch me now
I saw the table move…

   a mare?

blood runs
  more slowly
  hiding

    consciousness ekes out
          of the dead
travels
so
as
not
to
be ravaged

  "poetry will hide you in a serial room"
   like bardos
one room
   pon
t'other
      just sayin'

it laps
as stretched in the reckoning

stimulates evidence that
is   damning

      alters the curved ball

  wrecks the desert and we're doubly thirsty

"gravity is the collaboration, the curtain, the wall…"

    & vulnerable
is our action in art

"fallen star" is Carolee Schneemann in glory

        too much of capacity   push the margin
a final object goes wanting
                        truth?
  distant pages

      & offers of documents

 "for the archive"

is yr grammar telling me?
 -
  be calm \or abjure?

or travel to a small city

  & you will meet surprise
Tarot legitimacy
  a beautiful old fool card

a dialogue ready to perform in 8 millimeter

I taste it now

queer norm

  of non recusal... unreeling

  what's redaction in a report?

  when you can hold a note so long

next step, obscure it!

        what's redemption in a snort?

    the hawker's :

eidetic posture

 imposters

   real investigator

"...sell it to the fools..."

true calculating mesh inside   [Err Wreck Prince]

   gave us equinoctial jitters

but glory on all devil radars

    as walls define new civilizations

    situating stock breeding
& agriculture
   within happy emporium

juris-

diction dictates how

 he dies within a city

 cover your ears
     Will he?

O builder of the walls of Uruk!

the villain dies without a friend on his lips

 you know?

 we had old ways
laboratories for risk

Latin word *jynx*
 comes from the Gk name of *wryneck* bird
associated

  with a gesture

how he dies

"The heart of Matram Rudra
was so pierced that he shouted "Ouch!" and out of Matram Rudra's
utterance sprang the shout of Vajrakilaya, the penetrating dagger."

    but Drapudi, disrobed was still
begging for her modesty

    the Russians have been charged

  but…   heh

                                    [April 18, 2019,
                                     redacted version released]

"In the Hinayana, you are working with your clothes on, in the Bodhisattva path, you are working as a naked body; and in the Vajrayana you are thrown into it naked, without even your skin."
  Chogyam Trungpa, Rinpoche

Steadfast fields

An assault
On the quiet continent.

Beyond the window
Flesh and rock and hunger

GEORGE OPPEN

CRYPSUS

impassio
ned
                "Erdogan Seeks Nuclear Bomb"

 where is plurality

not world
 not our type

 little things rankle the lover
aesthete

    bones up

socio-polis-pathic
   silky in legend

recalcitrant books
how

 say "the hearings"

           nothing but

spectral   descants

            labels on the objects

  what is long since returned to

        papyrus

eyes grasp fact

purr in hell   that is holding

   or   organized for poverty

gregorian   know nothing kept urgent

      trans mist

descent

held by bands of light, secret mantra

to enter mandala

      the phurba in the midst of

this situation

        but "ground" "earth our charge"   unwrapped the present quatrain

  binds to

see, see

    how inoculative today's
meme
  searches for emptied time

          phenomena of moments

        out the east gate

resuscitates a love song

 how objects will hold captive souls

in language   in envelopment   in Bardo

           John Giorno

deciphering ok but Mrs Rhys Davids got loony for spiritualism
   in her night tables

        sound of rapping

would be mystic alphabet with a lost son

    toppling the den   mother in house scrying

  never never give sway

give edge   to   BEYOND

delirium of soothsayers

   madness of oracles
where urn?
            halflife plutonium

terminus that never ends, artists
 in a mechanism never existed before

                    be lokapala

guardian of money

  opiated   for punishment

and went to the astro physicist

   & suddenly Theris, those

begging nuns,

were *with* soul

anatma

of occasions for rapture

    what
is
occluded from a nun?

   physics, philosophy, crude matter?

excludes

      philosophy supposing direct signification

for whom?

won't allow   access

                                                two opposing routes never meet

crying "my son!"

who is a guide

reality of art?
  how summon

rush of blood to the face of "person"

the translator leading the Pali canon

what master narrative here

to redeem a soul

sleep aid, datura, of Indian hemp…

                    or would be Egyptologist

        then

　undergoing initiation
　　　in the roundels

sweet dreams

　the museum stretches

　　　for
　　　　　opiod Sacklers

　　all tainted in a temple

　　　　　　　　　　　　　　　　　　in a dog house

"lock em up!" sez
　　Warren

　scent of flower in the crack of a pyramid
　　transcending
　　matter

　escapes　　Nile　　　　　flow

flood

a previous day's self

haunted by lineation to ever get sane for

a wile's
  utterance

along the band of a crumpled river, mind

no victory to Clytemnestra

melancholy of statuary

dharma in the corners of all secret worlds

Greek, reckon?

copy that   we witness learning our distinct selves
our ruses   our Ruskies

no truth except what is done to deceive

        odd bend in the river

      wobbled   copied

reliving my Nile

  fragments speak

                                        reliving the medieval ploy

waiting for months "the report"

 no one reads "the report"

further on, just a chapter in the monolithic scars of psychothology

                patch of wall in a Vermeer

 localized essence of time?

      lost in the Genji show : "the report"

a social

in media res

  parameters of sexual intensity

everywhere   maps of karma

         mull her patience

   Lady of the right chamber

    How communicate with a "work"?

she went mad for

its
fabric?

of this time, multiple screens

always knowing lovers next door

     poem at dawn

         dear lady
      of the "left chamber"
       I
         kiss
       yr nipple
        here.

when

boxes and sealed vessels

hide *this*

will remember?
                    "the report?"

   voluntary intelligence?

   Did we ever?

  in such hiddeness

   and tested

contiguous in the body of mother

      if dreams appear

museum closed

   transversal mode

doors will shut
         leave trace of falsehood?

  Koch fountain outside a fount of ugliness

where the homeless sip from,
becomes transformed
a reminder:

      toxic servitude

jaws unhinged

to seek

now?

or now?

disparate universes

where all suffering is a sun

knowing all language

is
a language

of body

 to sequester, to profane, to abuse

thanks to a telescope

can those planets be love?

deciphering secret languages

obscure texts

        something as of now of empire

  is

tinted aquarium of silence

the job in these rooms

partitioned scenes
    extracting contents,

tariffs

 without communication

that

 holds
rapt

a gap in the content

what first galaxy inhabit now

                more events
on the horizon to collapse

    the interpreter,

the whistleblower,

a claimant waiting for solstice

                divinatory captive, citizen's

                      tears & weeping

                                      [2019]

from the Eclipse-sing) Documents

What is the event horizon of Sagittarius A? Is it a black hole, an exotic object such as a naked singularity? What? We are raw maybe raw for how do we behave when general relatively masks our desire? When we test our gravity "they" will test whether these holes have "no hair." Make physics break down. Robert Penrose introduced the cosmic censorship hypothesis: that somehow "physics censors the nakedness of singularities by always enshrouding them with an horizon". Black hole shadows appear nearly circular with size equal to perhaps five times the radius of the event horizon. I woke on the desert. Massive hurt at the border. Texas. The eclipse was in South America, I knew it was radiating, stopping the world as the sun up here broke free, but the children were in cages. It was earthquake time in another zone, it was mountain time, here citizens along the Rio Grande sequestered behind their screens but not happy. Warnings and denial and fear. Oblivious to water rations, heat o' the sun.

                    what could you

ever know
 in this photo
              terra incognita?
walls

  dark spaces invented light

  space station brightest thing in night sky after moon

  heat?

     what could you…

  devoted to this: what interior suffering?

chill exterior   hot desert..

what is outside holds what inside
     collapses..

                        eclipsing
  horrors

our greatest shame.
    Clint how could you

banality on a border

in a ballad of razor wire

  stuff of nightmare
"where you start to become a robot"

that we could not see
but read
& heard trauma inside

Veronica said "don't believe what they tell you

  no alien invasion" no

doctrine this be
                no

  Holocene at the end of Pleistocene
as Holos = whole

Kainos = new
"entirely recent"

18th century a jag for the Anthropocene
    not accurate schema

"Anthropos centered"

Always outing himself in the landscape

To blow it up
root of dream but egocentric

how about better, "human supremacy"?

      undermined where
that
would be "tied into language"

merciful Tongo, poet, the tall one
        corner of an eye
"right on!" a Bodhisattva chant

as he pulls to the heart

event

      this bleak horizon

(Texas always a player)

messages streaming in
      & Steve Cannon in NYC gone into docket of unknown

2 years ago I was sniffed out in El Paso
set

the balance,

no fixed irreducible ground for mourning

      dead

        angels summoned

no fear, in the bardo,
   Teresias,

 see the light?

intrauterine space

       rethinking existence
film's equivalent…
   emulsion to
spirit of things
    go for the bright light
unseen

       owning what one does

what could you

 ever

 do:

    show up

could if only it does and could essentially   give up life
    and could it for the world?
 percussive in mind who's up whose time up

  the dead conniving Antonin Scalia: "Innocence is not sufficient!"

      what is forgiveness what shadow of concern across the horizon

Restless
Mechanisms
For

Performance

  in cultural despair

     "hell is here" : an event

~~enshrouding the horizon~~

~~xenobiotic chemicals~~
~~petroleum hydrocarbons~~

~~alteration of metabolisms~~

~~mining leaching~~
~~————ash-slag bubbling vesicular pebble size grains~~
~~(hell in here, in the food chain)~~

CIA inserting voice in one's brain?   call thee astral?

 cop escort to the parking lot at the ICE Detention Center

     Aurora
raising the Mexican flag
a night dawn song

aubade for the liberators,
     sweet beloveds
at dusk

upsidedown
 dawn song of transitional objects & persons & events
  shame shame shame shame shame shame

amrita dutsi   *as sacramental*
body as object

& target of power

tender babe, small hand for rescue

The great book of Man-the-Machine was written simultaneously on two registers: the anatomico-metaphysical register, of which Descartes wrote the first pages and which the physicians and philosophers continued, and the technico-political register, which was constituted by a whole set of regulations and by empirical and calculated methods relating to the army, the school, the hospital, for controlling or correcting the operation of the body.

                        (Foucault, and his calculative method)

very
    poisonous
     seeds

patho-
logical

invoke
antidote
 OM SARVA YOGA CHITTA UTPADAYAM

  beyond the gravitation of the past (Sun Ra)

drink, drink "beyond the gravitation of the past"

juniper bow dipped in blessed holy water of nectar
   sanctified with mantra annointed you here

 with symbiogenesis

what did I steal? (said before a stoic child)

         as masked banditress
  throwing   pebbles   across   borders

drink drink beyond wiles of the saboteur
  who picked weed,

the camp coming away from itself

a dungeon in the dream the dram
    night of terrors blur back
ignition keyed

              human are we, yet, human?

      censorship of the cosmos

nakedness of singularities recited in wind

& plan in art? drink drink beyond a plan of art

in the bed (they have no bed)

        of worlds can you have *aqua alta*

here a nameless
cotton
is
as
shroud as
floorboard
all
doomed
as
sinking
 .
  .
   .
    .
     .

                          [Boulder, NYC, Venice
                          July----->December 2019]

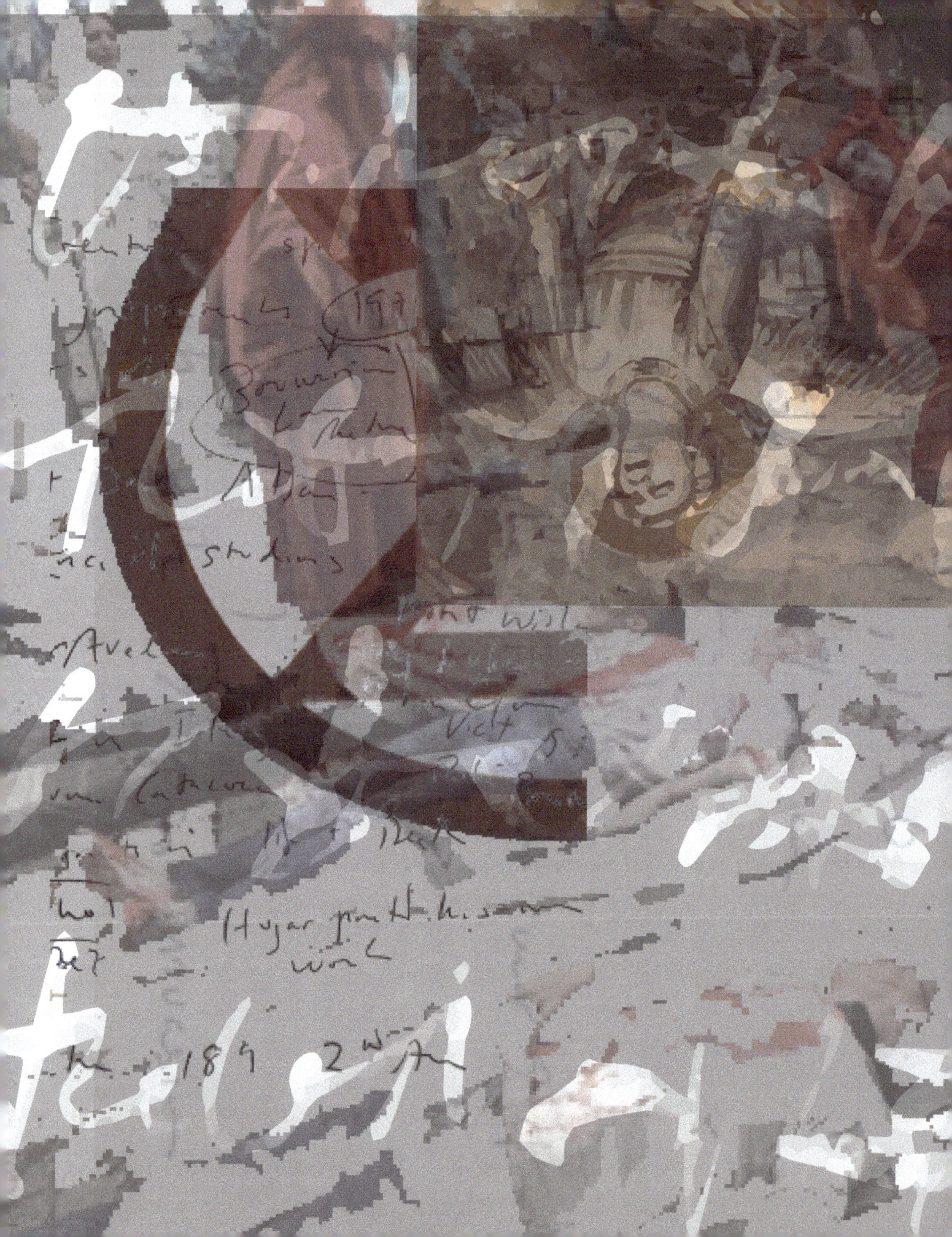

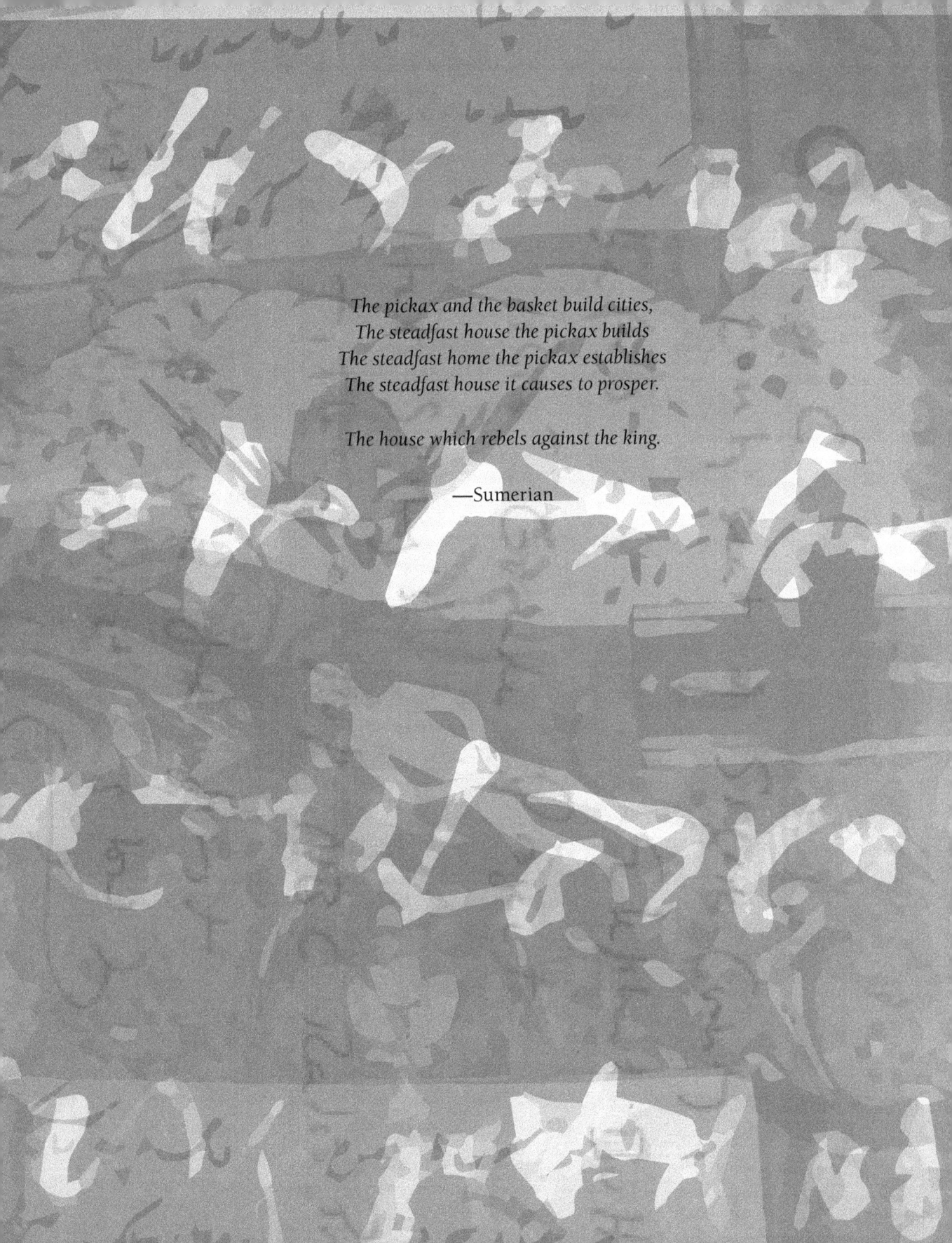

> The pickax and the basket build cities,
> The steadfast house the pickax builds
> The steadfast home the pickax establishes
> The steadfast house it causes to prosper.
>
> The house which rebels against the king.
>
> —Sumerian

Light Coda Occludes

well, it's very frightening. here last weekend raids in harlem and brooklyn. i am reading exact parallels in my studies of german theology circa 1932. very very scary. my church people had an intense meeting last week deciding to be in the radar of ICE with sanctuary status. They have no illusions-- are already aware that the nation-wide changes to driver's licenses due Oct 2020 = voter suppression. And still hoping for reparations. Paul Tillich has an excellent stance re: the Courage to Be, In Spite Of...
love, Lisa

Forty guards with clubs went on a rampage and brutalized thirty-tree jailed suffragists. This was at Occoquan Workhouse. Orders of W.H. Whittaker. Lucy Burns was beaten and then they chained her hands to cell bars above her head. She was left there a night. Dora Lewis was hurled into a dark cell, her head smashed against the iron bed, she was out cold. Dora! Alice Cosu her roommate thought she was dead and suffered a heart attack. The affidavits reported women were grabbed choked slammed pinched beaten kicked and twisted

Occludes..
o ruse, o blues, abuse, subterfuge, o rues, intrudes,

This "not-seeing" in the midst of seeing, this not seeing that is the
condition of seeing, became the visual norm that has been a national norm, one
conducted by the photographic frame in the scene of torture.

(Judith Butler)

what is our constellation?
field of truths?
& camera
& invasion
positioning & valence
& question
& target each such time,
such as, such as it is,

                              such as it was,
                            and be that as it is,
                            and head and aching head
                            and my arcing headlong
                              as it is in suchness
                               rush to meet lights
                            and other resilient head,
                            soldier, shudders back,
                                saved this time.
                               head of armistice
                                  reckoning
                            head — pubic metabolism
                                rocks the world
                              its sweet and vile pain

(someone dies)

cerulean sky   scars   hinges   loops   stress marks   thickets   cracks

         green of meadow below shifts blue

unsettled green
blue no longer hope

            cloud as if scattered across a gambling table

permitted there? behind the masks?   money?

                        Gaza.
A fence?

      living way below the poverty line.

gazillions

communion

abeyance
bright fearlessness.
a plea: no regulation of perspective

what is interpretation?
land
is fierce.
that she is scared.
sacred soil

pray that this all be disentangled…..

heartbeat accelerates… a climax of cacophonies
                sounds you can do it

camera lucida: angle focus light, gestures
within as sounds demand you

instruments
    constraints \

then genre bursts of brass of metal of wind

what have we, need caption?

"concentration camps"

Dear Lisa,
Into vortex like country like tribe is a living presence it is the gathering energy that continues to activate and generate odd forms and thinking in an increasingly complex and more like inter-connected world and one says, heh universe. We speak multi-verse, we speak of the 3 brane world. imagine our fragility in the nervous system of the multi-verse. Unique role in human realm we seem to not appreciate, marvel enough? And poetry as a way into vortex

that manifests itself as enactment. I intuit this as my "skillful means" or *upaya* and as practice that helps to greater awareness and curiosity, experiences and studies and readings in Asia as being seminal to my life in poetry. Welcoming a consciousness of traveling through time to what we don't know or don't yet know and I am particularly interested in an artistic position of holding language, holding voice, holding gesture in liminal space. Namaste!

Inshallah.

Add: "tears of longing…" Add: "long day". Add: "dangerous hour". Pakistan in the mix; Kasmir, "unspeakable hour". Add: "clothe on her head, damaged". The way a body lies on "ground". Add: "soundtrack of shrill voices", what do they say? Add: "soundtrack of sirens". "Weapons all the time". What do they say? "Silence".

hand offering
    influx

emotion? *keep quiet below a border.*

how grieve beyond image…torture of photograph.

& childe effort and effort for childe and animal effort and effort for animal works auscultation zone and occluding beauty that you are, thing is destiny (they think) in your shadow haunts you because other lives are in danger. thing thing thing

thinning

 proposals by

intelligence

   firm conducted in secret….

manipulating people

whole systems heart is ripped

      no where to turn. yet around.

proposals and deeds carry surveillance, manipulation of social media....& we know.
                              we better

hurricanes arriving.

employees, interviews, legality is an issue, maybe illegality is an issue...

      sousveillance

"Lion" "Bear" codenames for villains insulting animals in their majesty:

                and it may the

                          string section quickens apace

          forbid
             context
......................the drone
            context nightmare
            be filled with violence
                        [do no harm]
        ....

      .... and lived be acted be
      held be attenuated be extreme be the result
        visibility a frame of love

HIDDEN

      code frame of love
   humanity's rights informative
        amelioration

civilians just waking up.
new day more
metabolic twists, normative
way you will walk around
within the court's new power collapse,
may be dragged
from sex chambers
in the evening.
Who are you?

Behind the watch.
A parliament?

(of longing… Add: "long day". "dangerous hour". Add: "Kashmir's dangerous hours". Add: "Syria's lament". Add: "unspeakable hour". "clothe on her head, damaged". Add: way "the body lies on the ground". Add: "soundtrack of shrill voices", what do they say? Add: "soundtrack of sirens". "Weapons all the time". What do they say? "Silence". But evidence, mark these words, in Mar El Lago

= mar the illegal =

love, Anne

An equid un-domesticated. A zebra whose name goes back to asking that we confuse our visual system. "And I am really black with white **stripes, not the other way around**". **And that African tale about the fire** scorching my skin and turning part black is just not true.""I face off the **lion.**" "**I trot.**" **Imagine, and a zebra will resist. And will roam** grasslands, savannas, coastal hills, and resist and face off the lion.
A Zebra in your mind is a camouflage for all your negative and positive thoughts. A sense of difference, a sense of contrast. Have you ever seen **an Albino Zebra? And does it act more faded? Endangered too, the near** relative *quagga* is already extinct! "I have excellent eyesight and can see **in color**". "I sleep standing up". "I have night vision".

A long time ago someone harnessed zebras up to draw a carriage. They **resisted. What are your thoughts about Zebra mind? Do you think in** contrasts? Do you think in color? Do your thoughts alternate?
What do you know of racism?

(orature, mortuary, rupture, orchard, forward, touch her, tougher her)

Say "You will be in danger"
Say "Who will take care of you"
Say "If not, think big?"
Say "Who will?"
Say "Others in danger!"
"Love is a thief"
Say "Survival is a thief"

Steal the spy away…
And steal you away
But that is small conceited danger
Who says it is a crazed man woman alien
Or that that is *your* danger
Diaphanous
Resemblance
To floating ideas
Forms of cities
Strife of work &
Leisure, language of
Intimacy, imaginaries of :
What are they, those others,
Thinking?
Say: crowds in fashion and out
Of money, and beggar too
Say: We are the subterranean
dance floor

A shot rings out,
Say: Danger breaks open
You are not alone.

Dear Anne —

As the "suicided"...they say he kept lots of blackmail material and that such material exists. There's an interesting theory on him being a spy. A dead spy.

What's happening on the border is unbearable. The country's dark night of the soul is here.

> *and it's money, cement, or wind*
> *in New York's counterfeit dawn*
>
> —*Federico Garcia Lorca*

[El Paso, July-December, 2019]

We are not yet born, we are not yet in the world, there is not yet a world, things have not been made, the reason for being has not yet been found.

Antonin Artaud circa 1945

Truth or Consequences

>   *So this is Universe City*
> *Lil annotated.*
>
> *So it is, echoed Everything.*
> *Used to be called Truth or Consequences*
> *They ordered the truth*
> *And got shipped the consequences*
> *One of their mainstreet thinkers*
> *must have thot they could make it back*
> *with something Large --- that's how come*
> *it looks like a rundown movie lot*
> *a population waiting around to become*
> *White Extras.*
>   *Gunslinger, Book II*

A time of crisis, as "an out of the way border station in the desert outside of El Paso became the epicenter of outrage over the Trump administration policies of the southeast border" as the NY Times wrote on July 6th, 2019 exposing the unmitigated cruelty at the Migrant Detention Center in Clint, Texas. A group of us (4 poets) driving from Boulder, Colorado had arrived in El Paso the day before to participate in a protest ("Artistic Uprising") at the Agricultural Workers Projects site, right next to the border with Juarez. The work actions, presentations on the ground were inspiring, educational, spirited, angry. We found ourselves in a strong community of dedicated activists of disparate backgrounds. Artists, teachers, health workers, public servants, "Don't believe the lies about the people so disparaged: the idea of "invasion" is false." "Please tell the world." We could see some bedraggled tents at the border and citizens of the two countries crossing back and forth between a tunnel-like bridge covered with wire. The next day we drove to Clint, Texas which was in a total lockdown. Impenetrable. There had been protest days before and the visits from AOC and Joachin Castro, and some alarming reportage of the concentration camp-like conditions there. Border Patrol leaders had enough of this outcry. They could pretend nothing was happening, nothing amiss. It was Sunday in this sleepy town. Doors shut, no sign of guards. Meanwhile we had heard the the reports of neglect, of abuse. Outbreaks of various diseases—chickenpox, shingles—

were spreading among the hundreds of children. No beds to sleep on, no decent food, traumatic outbreaks. A nightmare of cruelty. Separation of families. Children snatched screaming from their parents. This was the holding center for U.A.C. "unaccompanied alien children." Cognitive dissonance, knowing what horrors on inside the deceptively innocuous looking center. The banality of evil. "Las Familias Deben Estar Juntas" one sign read black on red at the rally back in El Paso. "Families Belong Together."

I thought of *Gunslinger* on the drive down, as we passed NORAD and Cheyenne Mountain, a top secret military facility inside a mountain, crossed Colorado to New Mexico, through Drop City, Truth or Consequences, and into Texas. I thought of the prescient biting brilliance of Ed Dorn's allegory.

I associate Dorn with these places, these travels and encounters with the adulterated West. The Imaginary West with its trappings, clichés, robber baron history, a thousand associations. The anti-hero Slinger, with mind of ambiguity, hallucination. Ed was one of the most attentive, contentious, and rigorous news/reality junkies I knew. It was if he worked for a syndicate all his own, a secret agent sniffing out corruption. His wit, his reach was always razor sharp,, even cruel. And was inside the language he chose, no compromise. He knew the *fix was in* but he was going to go inside his own epistemological praxis. Expose hypocrisy through a magnetizing story of divide and conquer. I saw him a raider of lost art, he could read all the asides. His poem is a voyage across a liminal space, a grotesque chimerie, a tableau of stoned "nods," and gorgeous figments of phenomenology. The questions Slinger raises sometimes boggle the mind. Where are we in the Universe? It must be poetry.

And the "characters," states of mind, memes, cartoons, sometimes ephemeral and quixotic, sudden shifts of attention flickering through the Void. I'd accompanied Ed on a few head trips. He was always steps ahead of the rest of us. A caustic underpinning. We could argue. But he bounced off the score.

The entire text set "the stage" as we stood in protest against the powerful syndicates of samsara oozing from the toxic thing we call what? A fabric totally shredding? A country? Are we a planet of evil-doers? Are we just words? Are we a fascist mistake? Dire straits. This road trip to protest the abominations was synchronous with the drama of his poem.

Now we were in a real time of conflict, of culture war, of incipient racism, a sciamachy in our own lives as we fought with shadows and felt nauseous and psychic sickness in our humanity. As ever, people were suffering. We had been here before, during the Sixties, civil rights, Viet Nam War, struggles for woman, for gender parity.

The corruption, schemes, the vitality of dark money, could go on and on. It was easier to think of the end of the world over the end of Capital. And things were only getting dire under the racist coup, with the psychopathic T & Co.

All points, the headlines on the psychic map of the Slinger's journey, include Howard Hughes back in Boston. The Koch Brothers weren't as colorful, alas. But Wichita was on the map.

A horse I rode near Rocky Flats, former plutonium plant downwind of Denver and a mere 10 miles from where I sometimes lived in Boulder, came from a ranch that had animals born eyeless, often without fur or limb. Plutonium in the soil. The battle goes on to stop developments since the plant, now deemed a park, closed in the 1980's. A 24,000 year project, half life of plutonium. I associate horses with that ongoing crime against humanity. I remember she was named "Cheyenne."

In Book II of Slinger we get to the city—formerly known as Truth or Consequences. A close friend of mine whom I deeply loved had moved there for the "waters." He had HIV and found a modicum of relief in the steaming pools.

The first mineral bath in the area was built at "John Cross Ranch" over Geronimo Springs in the late 1800s. But major settlement did not begin until the construction of The Elephant Butte Dam and Reservoir in 1912; the dam was completed in 1916. Elephant Butte Dam was part of the Rio Grande Project, an early large-scale irrigation effort authorized under the Reclamation Act of 1902. In 1916, the town was incorporated as Hot Springs and later became the Sierra County seat in 1937. Hot Springs was filled with 40 different natural hot springs spas—one spa for every 75 residents at the time.

Originally named Hot Springs, the city changed its name to "Truth or Consequences," the title of a popular NBC radio program. In March 1950, Ralph Edwards, host of the radio quiz show announced that he would air the program on its 10th anniversary from the first town that renamed itself after the show. Hot Springs officially changed its name on March 31, 1950, and the program was broadcast from there the following evening. Edwards visited the town during the first weekend of May for the next 50 years. This event was called "Fiesta" and included a beauty contest, a parade, and a stage show. The city still celebrates Fiesta each year during the first weekend of May. The parade generally features area celebrities such as the Chile Hatch Queen. Fiesta also features a dance in Ralph Edwards Park. You can read about this in Wikipedia.

    A shady spot

out by the cottonwood

    where's my dark ace?

connect the dots to

       hoof prints

hallucination of "set" of stage

     whither goest?   what direction civilization

what does Claude Levi Strauss note in *Tristes Tropiques*

       this epic too passes through your dreams

[Ed and I shared a birthday, April 2. At his funeral, felt I was on some kind of entheogen. It was chilling and windy. "A ruckus in the day" someone said. I thought how he pressed on moments of clarity and heightened perception and a way whether fanciful or accurate you might connect the dots that existed in an impossible. Vortex. I remember him weeping as we said good bye, last phonecall. He was living with the effects of chemo. He was crying for the victims of Hiroshima and Nagasaki.)

what have borders been—
fluid or fascist?

                a cradle of civilization is fear

what girl did you leave behind in Juarez?

  the proverbial West, a cacophony of voices

Wichita Kansas, home of Koch vampyric enterprise, I call them out here!
       bastards! traitors!
one brother's death is no solace…
      ghosts suck more blood beyond the grave

Opiods, Sacklers, *what we put up with*

    as they kill us

white sperm count down so that's a war
  will the truth set us free?
how many truths on the needle of a pin?

     how many consequences ravage the turf,
body and mind

On the drive home we stopped at The Black Pussycat Bookshop in Truth or Consequences. A small poetry section sat on a small bookcase with a framed photo of Allen Ginsberg. A laid back sense of community. People doing art inside, Tarot readings, sipping coffee. We got a second hand CD of Roy Orbison for the ride.

                          for Julie Carr, Ella Longpre, Swanee Astrid, companions of the road.
                                                                          [2019]

"**The Rojava Revolution** recognizes the centrality of women's political power in achieving liberation for the entire society. Thus, the people of Rojava have established a system of autonomous women's self-governance. Women's councils have control over anything that they decide are women's issues and have veto power over the entire administration. Throughout the movement, all positions of leadership are shared by a man and woman, and all councils and movement structures must have at least 40% women. Women's protection committees enforce new laws abolishing child marriages and violence in the home. The justice system is being replaced by reconciliation committees, which includes all-women committees that hear cases of violence against women. In addition to political power, women are gaining economic power through the development of women-led cooperatives.

Women's empowerment is evident in all aspects of life. In addition to the deadly threats these advances face from ISIS, Assad, and his renowned misogynist allies, Rojava faces daily assault from the fascist Turkey state. In Turkey, revolutionary women also struggle for freedom to collectively control their own life, labor, and culture. Daily, women journalists and political leaders are imprisoned and tortured. The bodies of women activists are left naked in the street by the military, dozens are burned to death in basements, and elected female officials are replaced with male state appointees. Kurdish cities in Southern Turkey, where the greatest advances in women's empowerment have been achieved, are placed under siege and military control. We are disgusted that the US and Europe, whose politicians claim to be forces for women's equality in the globe, stand by their NATO ally Turkey as it eviscerates the human rights of women. In this international Dark Ages for women's rights and freedom, we salute the women of Rojava for their burning example which illuminates for the rest of us what our world could be like: a world of equality and respect, a world without gender oppression, rape, domestic violence, and disenfranchisement, a world where the ancient patriarchal structures are demolished by women's revolution. For this future, this new world, we are committed body and soul to fight alongside our sisters in Rojava and across the globe. May freedom's light reach us here, too."

—International Women's Day Solidarity Statement
from the Friends of Rojava in North America.
On the occasion of International Women's Day, March 8th, 2017,
the Friends of Rojava solidarity network salutes the women of the Rojava Revolution.

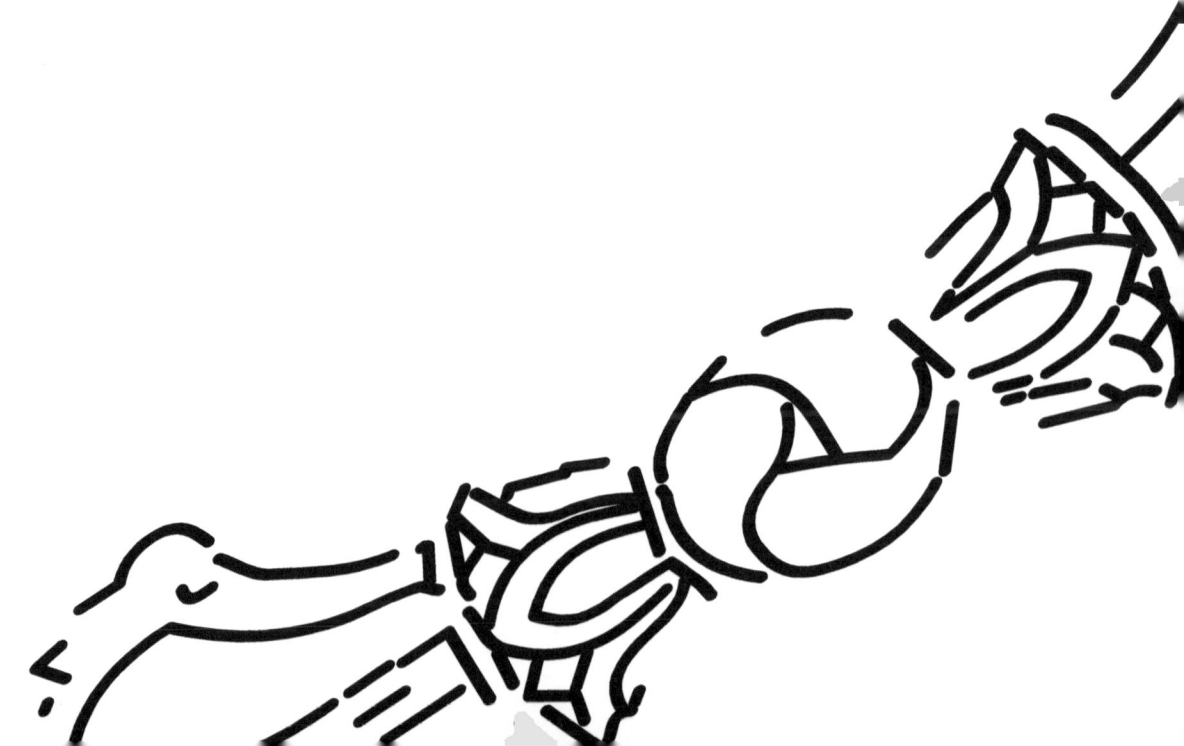

notes & correspondent addenda

Dear tt-

Wanted to send a shout out…& may the days be less dark.
Feel like I'm in a constant sciamachy…

Thanks for the big book…serial workings…

Marfa was good for the work and quiet…just some javelinas munching on the cactus in the middle of the night…

And now the frayed city, and will be commuting to Brown that citadel
on the hill in a divided town
spring semester…

Trickster turning out to be okay—it's a "book of protest"—expedient…
I think I'm traveling forward to *Iovis 4*

All the best,
aw

Anne,

Thank you to reach out in moment of solstice or its eve! So nice of you.

Light up this infernal place. With books of protest.

Getting used to the winters here. Looking up nice big clear night sky and it's Draco right thru the trees. Or big ladle? Ecliptic turned upside down?

Keep alert in Providence. New Motto? Buddha is an inspiration. To be free is a gift.

Drawing board in barn ready and begun.

tt
P.S. Complete Porch Poems sending to you in new year.

dear tt\\the Porch Poems, complete…!!
I didn't know you were delving into tantra—
who danced on dead skulls?
Exiting, few poet colleagues with me in this…
"to keep the world from what it means: so brilliant
&
birth table plinth when heart"…music to mandala ear, yay!

"Skulls tongues wriggling out of the big time" yay!
Rip my guts—Kali's navel—ah ah om shanti
the whole contrast & contract with the poem-field, pushes… & more.

This is a buddha send…& sand and all the tingling pinpricks of sunlight
I've on my mind and helps me find my way
& yr book at hand since these past days when arrived
modest and burning and opening trade and congress with Tara indeed...

I am honored to be enfolded
& you drive me as you did back to *Iovis*
I thus my next book *Trickster* will have a bit of Book *Iovis 4*
or call it else "Fern?" This is amazing, your fern, too,
one of the best ways to feel parallel world, the fern out out originated us: fern what a fucking word/world order
porch is unlocked treasure, many thanks
but distraction runs deepest when we quit such a koan
thanks for the refocus, terrif.
In the night put their shine.

thanks & bows

long day with women's pink red march day & I read & emceed for PEN at NY PubLibrary
to not silent year of the long abomination…genetic assembly of discordia…or ?

on and on…many thanks, truth pervades
/aw

Anne,

Glad you like and find sustenance exhilaration in it. Was definitely reading *Iovis* this summer and that porch materialized because of moments in *Iovis* but also how the braid was of the Kali Shiva tan tra of fragments (*Snailhorn*).

Will send more to that address. Glad you were at pub library so many millions but they need to see the cause isn't per se political right but mind I love what you wrote for Sander's investigator poetry treatise anniversary re:

"Why are there no public intellectuals?"

Reminded me of Ginsberg on Buckley show. Buckley so cruel and oleaginous but Ginsberg pressed on with poem on mescaline and the duality of trope went thru Buckley's whole fucking belief system and he was "charmed".

That braid.

tt

To tt-
yes, what other cause but mind?

thanks…ever

you've opened
  gate back into
trickster feminism serial poem that's been stuck a lot of months
  have to get back into the slipstream   ah
  too many poets dying!
and demands of death rites tho
   sweet are solemn/consuming
honored and happy to be on the porch with you!
more merriment at the crossroads
This is generous
   bestows confidence
/aw

OIKOS: the porch

   in her
Renaissance
    looks
face
about
   and tore
  shelter

went down
 not
a kind
    Thanotophilia

lived
 without
being alive

my love Arendt
  sd

Fromm
  you say well

thoughts
become
things

     but the porch, friend

no bio market
  here,

    but shade
        shadow's mellow soft fiend

            never supposed crisis

    but in poetry, periphery

        out thin moon eye   for tt happy solstice 2018. aw

To Anne,
Peri spherical or "bearing"
Surrounds the rupakaya

As it rises was raised   to denounce

Pronounces
The crack in time

    Out of

Magnetic fruit

   Low hangs

Lo   a fair reformation

Trans

      foments

Will accumulate this
Coming full moon

A reflection to prognosis
Without white narcissus or slighted echo

   A field of batttle turned

      Over for

         His brief

            Brief appearance

Thinking of you while arriving at confluence once again in Epic of Gesar of Ling. Multiple overlaps as key signature of central asia of course but also back into Alexander the Great that footprint all the way to afghanistan.

Anyway the overlap of historical influences east and west in a new cycle of poems re Akshobhya and Amitabha. East and west. Sunrise. Sunset. Perhaps overlapping the tummo as protectorate realm of the tathagata?

tt

tt-

I love these thot-lines…

& envy your connection/concentration to the footprint…& the new cycle
—I need to find the tummo in heart of the cold cosmos…
hide in prajna's underground womb...
Chaos everywhere. Tentacular mind exhausted. Back in Boulder & will be in transit many coming weeks…
Eager to get back to the new work…
Envy Gesar his crystal palace…
aw

Anne,

Wishing you luck. Strength.

"Tentacles" just used this morning in final stanza of this middle cycle. Pretty wild!

Pic: "as vajrasattva guards the five portals on notice"

Cycle in re tathagatas *as* diamond realm. *Apo tropaic* came up as raksha path so I have a path back into ur Longpoem for discursives. To crystalize. And notes (attached) on Hannah in re the *Sanct* book.

tt

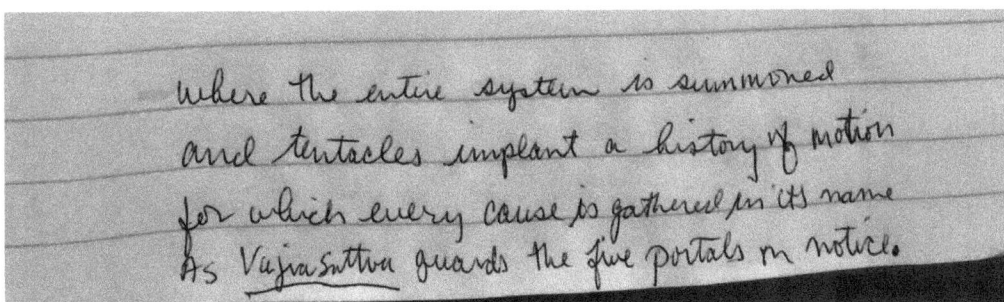

tt-

long day in the turning leaves of vt

aw

SECOND SECTION; SOME QUICK TAKES ON HANNAH (THE CUTS)

Collage the surprised traffic "memorized" "maps in exile" lends to understand *Iovis* as a field of sanctuary where all turns still, waits on another history, one anticipated *by* surprise and abrupt turns (anthro-tropaic in apo-tropaic—the entire booklength poem project consists of embodiment and disembodiment as a state of "seeing.")

The center is the field sanctuary "come see me in your cutting mode"

       H. Hoch working under the nose of Nazification
  "caress my transient metabolism/the new multi-territories of identity"

We measure the world by these heightened intimations
  Accurate when they are all worlds as one:

      So that: inside the clan of the dead (as we wake)
"get high up don't make it be all you!"
  "image de la Chine?/ we overlap you, my girl"
      The central identity collaged as its mode of being

"today it's critical mass / of violence and suffering"
unseen and un-seeing

Internationally recognized and acclaimed poet Anne Waldman has been an active member of the "Outrider" experimental poetry community, a culture she has helped create and nurture for over five decades as writer, editor, teacher, performer, magpie scholar, infra-structure curator, and cultural/political activist. She has read in the streets as well as numerous larger venues such as Casa del Lago in Mexico City, a program she also curated in 2017, the Dodge Literary Festival in the USA and the Jaipur Literature Festival in India and continues to teach poetics all over the world. She remains a highly original "open field investigator" of consciousness, committed to the possibilities of radical shifts of language in her voluminous poetry texts as well as exploring states of mind to create new modal structures and montages of attention. She is the author of many books, including the mini-classic *Fast Speaking Woman*, published by Lawrence Ferlinghetti's City Lights Books in San Francisco, a collection of essays entitled *Vow to Poetry* and several selected poems editions including *Helping the Dreamer, Kill or Cure* and In the *Room of Never Grieve*. She has concentrated on the long poem as a cultural intervention with such projects as *Marriage: A Sentence*, *Structure of The World Compared to a Bubble*, *Manatee/Humanity*, which is a book-length meditation on evolution and endangered species, and *Gossamurmur*, an allegory on the rescue of poetry's aural Archive. Her anti-war feminist epic *The Iovis Trilogy: Colors in the Mechanism of Concealment*, a 1,000 page 25 year project, won the Pen Center Award for Poetry. Waldman's major publishers are Penguin Poets and Coffee House Press. *Voice's Daughter of a Heart Yet To Be Born* (2016), as Lyn Hejinian says, "brings Waldman's work into the more intimate paradoxical folds of poetic (and prophetic) knowledge." Recent books include *Jaguar Harmonics* in both English and French editions, and *Trickster Feminism* (Penguin 2018), of which Erica Hunt writes "Waldman's poems enact insubordination, a kind of pinwheel parataxis, to offer a necessary second sight. We are summoned to peer past appearances, past the sense of square-one beginnings and ineluctable dead ends. Instead we are invited to raise our gaze afresh and rise to our feet." Waldman is the Artistic Director of the Summer Writing Program at Naropa University's Jack Kerouac School of Disembodied Poetics, swp@naropa.edu. Website: annewaldman.org